# ANIMAL
# TOTEM
# ASTROLOGY

# ANIMAL TOTEM ASTROLOGY

Uncover your unique
relationship to nature
and the seasons

DEBBIE BURNS

LANSDOWNE

# CONTENTS

# INTRODUCTION

## WHY ANIMAL TOTEM ASTROLOGY?

This book uncovers for you the secrets and essential aspects of animal totem astrology. In this ancient system, practiced by American Indians in the past and today, an animal totem is an animal, fish or bird chosen to represent a particular time of birth, season of birth, or element of nature. Knowing about your animal totem can give you insight into your own nature. In times of trouble, associating yourself with the animal totems of other people will allow you to take on the characteristics of others and understand more about yourself.

As with most systems, variations exist. Some tribes in the vast territory of the Americas have differing totems for time of birth, the seasons and/or the elements. This book presents the most common and more widely known of the animal totems.

### ANIMAL TOTEM ASTROLOGY TODAY

You will find the animal totem astrological system both relevant and useful no matter where in the world you were born or where you are living today. The totems and affinities still hold their power regardless of your distance from the natural home of the American Indians.

Knowing your totem animal, and the nature of the other totem animals, will help you to:
• understand your own personality as well as your relationship with others, nature, and the earth and its seasons
• answer your questions about the path you are meant to travel in your life
• identify the totems and affinities that will support you and help you to stay balanced in a chaotic world, and offer protection from harm
• build rapport and maintain harmonious relationships with others.

## How to Use this Book

This book is a resource tool for those interested in American Indian beliefs, culture and practices, particularly as these relate to astrology and its place in our lives. We begin with **An overview of American Indian Culture and Beliefs**, such as the shaman and the Medicine Wheel, to help you to understand the origins and principles of animal totem astrology.

In **Finding Your Animal Totem**, information is given to:
• guide you to your specific animal totem, based on your season of birth
• outline the key influences of nature's elements on your animal totem, and your totem's natural group memberships with other animal totems.

**Animal Totem Profiles** give details of the twelve animal totems:
• their unique personality traits, elements and energy types
• the gifts of each animal type and the challenges they face in terms of difficult areas of personality
• life path — what each animal type should constantly bear in mind about the correct approach to life
• affinities from the plant and mineral kingdoms: for each animal totem, there is a specific plant and mineral that share its characteristics, and provide additional strength and healing powers for the animal totem.

The section **Influences of the Element and Seasons** will give you more information on:
• the way the elements of nature help to define your personality
• your natural kinship with other animal totems, based on the elements and seasons you share.

In **Animal Totem Pairings — Relationships and Challenges** discover:
• your relationship strengths with other animal totems, and possible challenges in difficult pairings.

# AN OVERVIEW OF AMERICAN INDIAN CULTURE AND BELIEFS

## THE ORIGINS OF ANIMAL TOTEM ASTROLOGY

Animal totem astrology originates in the beliefs and customs of American Indians. Long before the arrival of the white man, American Indians thrived in tribes found throughout the Americas, including the present-day United States, Canada and Mexico. Among the common ideological elements was the belief that all life on the earth, in the water world and in the sky and heavens has a spiritual essence. All living things in these worlds, whether animal, plant or mineral, was said to possess a spiritual core, a unique and intangible 'power.' And all living things collectively formed one Great Spirit — the spirit of all life. These beliefs are still strong today.

LIFE'S TRUE PURPOSE AND HARMONY: American Indians believe the purpose of life for each individual is to find and keep to a particular spiritual path. This can only be achieved by living each day in conscious awareness of your thoughts, words and deeds. American Indians believe true harmony in life comes from appreciating and paying homage to everything on the earth, in the water and in the skies. The animals, fish and birds are seen to hold great power — power to communicate messages between the natural and the spiritual worlds.

NATURE AND HUMAN PERSONALITY: Native Americans draw many parallels between nature and the seasons and the elements of human personality. These parallels provide specific guidelines for maintaining optimal physical, emotional and psychological health, and for the medicine required if disease occurs. Their knowledge of nature and the seasons also enables Native Americans to make prophecies for the future of the tribe as a whole.

# THE SHAMAN

In American Indian tribal life, wise men, called shamans, have always been held in special reverence. Shamans are believed to have the power to recognize the intricate relationship between the natural and supernatural worlds, and to draw conclusions for the person or group involved.

For instance, by looking at each seasonal period and the particular animals, colors, stones and plants that have an affinity with this period, shamans can make accurate descriptions of people's characters and purpose in life. This information can then be used as powerful medicine for individuals looking for advice on current troubles, and for supporting people on their life's journey.

HEALING WITH THE MEDICINE WHEEL: The shamans use symbolic ornaments and totems to help individuals to understand themselves and others. They have integrated all the seasonal birth times with their symbolic ornaments and totems in a Medicine Wheel. This is illustrated on page 11. Using the Wheel, shamans demonstrate how harmony and balance can be achieved among all elements of life on earth. They can also show how everything has its place in tribal life and in the world of the land, seas and skies as a whole. Ill fortune will come if the balance is disrupted.

USING THE BIRTH TIMES FOR HEALING: Each of the twelve birth times also provides distinct gifts and talents that a shaman can use to heal the troubles of their people. For example, people born during the dead of winter, that is, the cleansing time, are said to be closely connected with the life spirit, and to have prophetic powers, and, at the very least, latent healing powers. A person in pain, either physically or spiritually, would be advised to spend time with someone born during the cleansing period. Also, at times when it is necessary to look ahead to the future to seek answers to present dilemmas, the tribal shaman will call on the totems and affinities of the cleansing period for assistance.

# THE MEDICINE WHEEL

The table lists the core elements of the traditional Medicine Wheel.

| Direction, season totem, season element | Season | Time of year | Birth totem | Birth time element |
| --- | --- | --- | --- | --- |
| North/White Buffalo AIR | Winter | Renewal | Snow Goose | Earth |
| | | Cleansing | Otter | Air |
| | | Strong winds | Wolf | Water |
| East/Eagle FIRE | Spring | Budding | Hawk | Fire |
| | | Growing | Beaver | Earth |
| | | Flowering | Deer | Air |
| South/Coyote WATER | Summer | Long days | Woodpecker | Water |
| | | Ripening | Salmon | Fire |
| | | Harvesting | Brown Bear | Earth |
| West/Grizzly Bear EARTH | Autumn | Falling leaves | Raven | Air |
| | | Frosting | Snake | Water |
| | | Long nights | Owl | Fire |

A note on the compass directions: These represent affinities with elements of life. North represents darkness and is hence associated with winter, whereas south represents light, and is hence associated with summer, a time of long days. Animal totems with the direction north — the winter totems — would be those with a more introspective, spiritual nature, as the coldness of the winter season would cause people to spend more time indoors, and less time engaged in physical activities in the world outside.

Note also that the S at the center of the Wheel represents the never-ending flow of energy, the life force.

# THE MEDICINE WHEEL

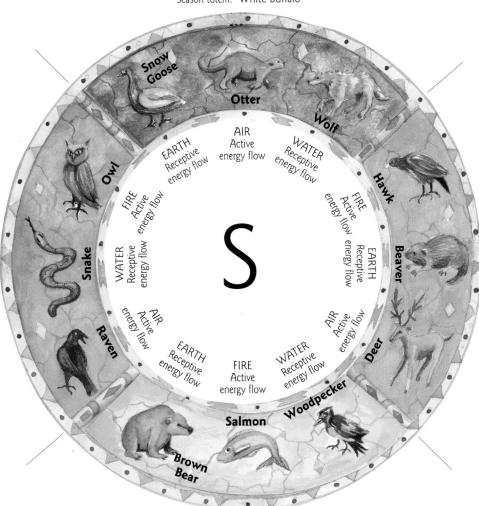

**NORTH**
WINTER
Season element: AIR
Season totem: White Buffalo

**EAST**
SPRING
Season element:
FIRE
Season totem:
Eagle

**WEST**
AUTUMN
Season element:
EARTH
Season totem:
Grizzly Bear

**SOUTH**
SUMMER
Season element: WATER
Season totem: Coyote

Snow Goose

Otter

Wolf

Owl

Snake

Raven

Hawk

Beaver

Deer

Woodpecker

Salmon

Brown Bear

EARTH
Receptive
energy flow

AIR
Active
energy flow

WATER
Receptive
energy flow

FIRE
Active
energy flow

FIRE
Active
energy flow

EARTH
Receptive
energy flow

WATER
Receptive
energy flow

AIR
Active
energy flow

AIR
Active
energy flow

EARTH
Receptive
energy flow

FIRE
Active
energy flow

WATER
Receptive
energy flow

S

# FINDING YOUR ANIMAL TOTEM

## ANIMAL TOTEM BASED ON SEASON OF BIRTH

American Indians drew many parallels between nature and the seasons and the elements of human personality. They believed that the season in which you were born influenced your personality. Use this table to find your birth totem — your animal totem based on the seasonal period in which you were born. Details are given for both the northern and the southern hemispheres.

| Season of birth | Time of year | Birth totem | N. hemisphere | S. hemisphere |
|---|---|---|---|---|
| Early winter | Renewal | Snow Goose | 12/22–1/19 | 6/21–7/22 |
| Winter | Cleansing | Otter | 1/20–2/18 | 7/23–8/22 |
| Late winter | Big winds | Wolf | 19/2–20/3 | 23/8–22/9 |
| Early spring | Budding | Hawk | 3/21–4/19 | 9/23–10/22 |
| Spring | Growing | Beaver | 4/20–5/20 | 10/23–11/21 |
| Late spring | Flowering | Deer | 5/21–6/20 | 11/22–12/21 |
| Early summer | Long days | Woodpecker | 6/21–7/22 | 12/22–1/19 |
| Summer | Ripening | Salmon | 7/23–8/22 | 1/20–2/18 |
| Late summer | Harvesting | Brown Bear | 8/23–9/22 | 2/19–3/20 |
| Early autumn | Falling leaves | Raven | 9/23–10/22 | 3/21–4/19 |
| Autumn | Frosts | Snake | 10/23–11/21 | 4/20–5/20 |
| Late autumn | Long nights | Owl | 11/22–12/21 | 5/21–6/20 |

# Essential Information about Your Birth Totem

| Animal totem | Season element | Season totem | Birth time element | Elemental clan | Energy flow |
|---|---|---|---|---|---|
| Snow goose | Air | White buffalo | Earth | Turtle | Receptive |
| Otter | Air | White buffalo | Air | Butterfly | Active |
| Wolf | Air | White buffalo | Water | Frog | Receptive |
| Hawk | Fire | Eagle | Fire | Thunderbird | Active |
| Beaver | Fire | Eagle | Earth | Turtle | Receptive |
| Deer | Fire | Eagle | Air | Butterfly | Active |
| Woodpecker | Water | Coyote | Water | Frog | Receptive |
| Salmon | Water | Coyote | Fire | Thunderbird | Active |
| Brown bear | Water | Coyote | Earth | Turtle | Receptive |
| Raven | Earth | Grizzly bear | Air | Butterfly | Active |
| Snake | Earth | Grizzly bear | Water | Frog | Receptive |
| Owl | Earth | Grizzly bear | Fire | Thunderbird | Active |

For more information on the significance of the seasons and their totems, and the elements and their clans, see 'Season elements,' pages 42–43; 'Season totems,' pages 48–51; and 'Elemental clans,' pages 52–55.

For more information on energy flow types, see the section 'Animal totem profiles,' pages 14–39.

# ANIMAL TOTEM PROFILES

In the belief system of the American Indians, each birth-time totem is not complete unto itself; each relies on the others for wholeness and balance. Some of the totems complement others; for example, some have an active energy flow, and some a receptive energy flow. This means that some signs are more introspective, others more outward-looking.

Apart from unique gifts and attributes, each birth time also brings specific challenges to those born during its time. The attributes, gifts, traits and challenges combine to outline each individual's purpose in life.

# THE SNOW GOOSE

**Season:** Early winter — a time when nature comes to rest and to renew itself

**Season totem:** White Buffalo

**Season element:** Air

**Birth time:** 12/22–1/19 northern hemisphere

6/21–7/22 southern hemisphere

**Birth time element:** Earth

**Elemental clan:** Turtle

**Energy flow:** Receptive

**Affinities:** Color: white

Plant: birch tree

Mineral: quartz

**Gifts:** Gregariousness, enthusiasm, idealism, determination, perseverance, respect, thoroughness, seriousness, realism

**Challenges:** Skepticism, arrogance, stubbornness, authoritativeness

**Life path:** To let go and be open to the new and unknown; to spend some time outside of the usual routine, with no structure or expectation.

## Snow Goose People

The Snow Goose, a beautiful white bird with black-tipped wings, is quite gregarious, living and traveling in a large flock. Its migration pattern encompasses flying off to northern nesting grounds just as spring begins and returning with the first snows of late autumn/early winter. This is a sign to American Indians to prepare for the coming winter, an intense season requiring rest, cleansing and renewal of the spirit. Snow Geese are referred to as the 'birds beyond the north winds.'

Snow Goose people are referred to as the 'keepers of old wisdoms.' They are traditional, ritualistic and serious, sometimes appearing proper, stately and even reserved. However, they do like to be around others, provided social gatherings are for constructive purposes as well as opportunities for exercising their intelligence.

They have a strong code of conduct and keen vision, which ensures that they are meticulous and thorough in everything in which they are involved. They set high standards of performance for both themselves and others, and at times can come across as nit-picking and manipulative.

Snow Goose people are loyal, respecting their family members, friends and work colleagues. They can truly keep confidences, and will stand by and support family, friends and colleagues through the roughest and darkest of times.

Some Snow Goose people have a talent for story-telling. With their vivid imagination and ability to communicate clearly and concisely, they have the attributes for communicating in story form the ideals and customs that mean so much to them.

# THe OTTeR

**Season:** The heart of winter — a time of cleansing, purification and reflection
**Season totem:** White Buffalo
**Season element:** Air
**Birth time:** 1/20–2/18 northern hemisphere
7/23–8/22 southern hemisphere
**Birth time element:** Air
**Elemental clan:** Butterfly
**Energy flow:** Active
**Affinities:** Color: silver/grey
Plant: aspen tree
Mineral: silver

**Gifts:** Imaginativeness, humanitarianism, youthfulness, perceptiveness, curiosity, empathy, passion
**Challenges:** Sensitivity, idealism, impracticality, intensity
**Life path:** To develop your latent psychic powers consciously, maintain an easy flow of emotion, and regularly touch base with the physical world around you.

## Otter People

American Indians view the Otter as one of the most playful and friendly animals in the wild. Otters appear to live their lives in true bliss. Relaxing and sunning themselves one moment, next moment they are quickly attending to the chores of hunting and eating before moving on to play and cooling themselves in water. Like their animal totem, Otter people are clever and gentle and have keen intellects, as well as a playful, inquisitive approach to life and a sociable nature. Like their metal and color affinity, silver, Otter people are shiny, flexible and beautiful to behold. They are viewed as precious additions to a family and community due to their dynamism and their ability to attract good fortune and abundance.

Otter people possess strong powers of perception, intuition and vision. They display true affection for others, with flowing emotional energy that can make them passionate and ardent lovers. Otter people often have psychic abilities, with a knack for accurately predicting the future.

Otter people make good friends and lively companions, particularly during hard times, as they act as motivators and uplift the mood and outlook of everyone around them. Rarely judgmental, Otter people are open-minded, empathetic, tolerant, light-hearted and generous, and follow the call to humanitarian causes in their choice of career.

Otter people adapt easily to new people and surroundings, and prefer to live life at a lively pace. They are independent, individualistic and true extroverts, which is reflected in their active energy type. They need only rare moments of solitude in order touch base effectively with their feelings and spirituality.

# THE WOLF

**Season:** Late winter — a time of big, strong, blustery winds
**Season totem:** White Buffalo
**Season element:** Air
**Birth time:** 2/19–3/20 northern hemisphere
8/23–9/22 southern hemisphere
**Birth time element:** Water
**Elemental clan:** Frog
**Energy flow:** Receptive
**Affinities:** Color: blue-green
        Plant: plantain
        Mineral: turquoise

**Gifts:** Creativity, intuitiveness, trustworthiness, loyalty, philosophical nature, spirituality, genuineness, selflessness
**Challenges:** Restlessness, depression, nervousness, indecisiveness
**Life path:** To harness the emotional winds that can buffet you in many different physical directions, and make you subject to many different moods.

## WOLF PEOPLE

American Indians admire the Wolf, seeing it as a fine example of the successful integration of individualism and family unity. Wolves live in family packs in which clearly defined roles are respected, yet they will also strike out on their own, exploring new terrain for a while before returning to the pack. Witnessing a wolf howling at the moon is a message to turn within and seek harmony and your spiritual connections.

Wolf people are prone to contradictions in their characters. For instance, they may become restless if little or no individual space and freedom are provided. They may also become stressed and worried if left on their own for too long. It's a constant tug-of-war that Wolf people impose on themselves — a struggle between freedom and independence, and home and security. This struggle is characterized by the season of their birth — late winter is a time of big, blustery winds.

Among some of the gifts Wolf people possess are their incredibly keen senses. Their finely tuned instincts and keen sense of their environment and the people around them enable them to pick up messages very swiftly. If something or someone doesn't feel right, Wolf people will quickly back away, often without being able to tell what it is that is making them feel uneasy.

Wolves are sensitive, and can easily take offense and be hurt by the actions and words of others. This is particularly evident in their love life, which can be rocky at times. They need to temper this by seeking clarification and confirmation of others' intentions, and by trying to control their reactions more carefully.

# THE HAWK

**Season:** Early spring — a time of birth, of new life and budding, and of awakening from winter's hibernation
**Season totem:** Eagle
**Season element:** Fire
**Birth time:** 3/21–4/19 northern hemisphere
9/23–10/22 southern hemisphere
**Birth time element:** Fire
**Elemental clan:** Thunderbird
**Energy flow:** Active
**Affinities:** Color: yellow
        Plant: dandelion
        Mineral: opal

**Gifts:** Foresight, energy, optimism, perceptiveness, boldness, honesty, sincerity, independence
**Challenges:** Rashness, willfulness, impatience, impulsiveness
**Life path:** To pace oneself in everyday life and reflect more on the likely outcomes of one's actions before taking the initiative.

22

# HAWK PEOPLE

American Indians believe that Hawks are Messengers of the Sky. Sighting one or hearing its cry is an omen of new arrivals or new things about to happen, either good or bad. Hence seeing or hearing a Hawk signals the need to become more aware of the environment, and to be prepared for change.

Hawk people are often seen as the messengers of insight and the seekers of truth, demonstrating keen perceptiveness and foresight in their daily lives as well as in the lives of others. Nothing escapes their x-ray vision; nothing can quench their determination to uncover the truth in all matters.

Hawks are 'big-picture' people, who need to see the overall plan before they can attend to minute details. However, once they are committed to an overall plan, Hawks can easily apply their acute perception to even minor aspects, ensuring that few, if any, details are left unattended.

Action-oriented, bold and quick, given their active energy-flow type, Hawks prefer initiating new ideas and projects rather than attending to completion. Once things are up and running, they prefer to lead others, getting them to attend to day-to-day routine activities and completion.

Hawks often fly from one project to another quite quickly, as this suits their lightning-fast minds and physical momentum. However, as this swift energy comes only in short bursts, long-range projects are best avoided. Hawks readily and quite naturally embrace change.

# THE BEAVER

**Season:** The heart of springtime — a time of rapid growth

**Season totem:** Eagle

**Season element:** Fire

**Birth time:** 4/20–5/20 northern hemisphere
10/23–11/21 southern hemisphere

**Birth time element:** Earth

**Elemental clan:** Turtle

**Energy flow:** Receptive

**Affinities:** Color: blue
Plant: lily
Mineral: turquoise

**Gifts:** Tenacity, practicality, steadfastness, industriousness, patience, reliability, dexterity

**Challenges:** Over-indulgence, stubbornness, opinionatedness, inflexibility

**Life path:** To embrace emotions readily and express them constantly, thus avoiding a totally logical approach to life.

## Beaver People

Beavers are viewed by Native Americans as nature's prime example of industriousness. Beaver dams are engineering feats, cleverly created to provide the animal with many entries and exits so it is secure from its enemies.

Beavers spend much of their time working on their dams, and little time at play. Beaver people are extremely practical, hard-working individuals who demonstrate an almost unlimited abundance of patience, whether at work on individual tasks or in the company of others.

They expect high standards of performance from themselves and others. Yet they are not stressed by deadlines, as they apply themselves methodically, and commit others to a clear action plan that will get everyone there in the end. Beavers are extremely task-focused, operating at the material level. Hence, they don't come across as big talkers, travelers or socializers.

Beavers' families and homes are extremely important to them. They will readily commit whatever is required — money, time or anything else — in order to make their hearth secure.

Their energy type is reflective, which means they like to think before they act. They have the capacity to embrace the emotional, nurturing side of life; Beavers do feel deeply about their lives and the people in them. However, they can have a difficult time expressing and demonstrating their feelings.

# THE DEER

**Season:** Late spring — a time of expansion and flowering, of color and beauty

**Season totem:** Eagle

**Season element:** Fire

**Birth time:** 5/21–6/20 northern hemisphere
11/22–12/21 southern hemisphere

**Birth time element:** Air

**Elemental clan:** Butterfly

**Energy flow:** Active

**Affinities:** Color: green
        Plant: yarrow
        Mineral: moss agate
        (a type of quartz)

**Gifts:** Grace, gentleness, sensitivity, beauty, versatility, alertness, intuitiveness, wittiness, joviality

**Challenges:** Nervousness, restlessness, disorganization, talkativeness

**Life path:** To take life more seriously when necessary and to focus on preparation and organization in daily life.

## DEER PEOPLE

Deer are beautiful to behold, and American Indians have esteemed them for this quality, as well as for their natural grace, gentleness and agility. To come upon a deer or fawn was a sign for the American Indian that you should stop, and appreciate the beauty and love you have in your life.

Deer people are beautiful both physically and spiritually, as they radiate love and concern for others in all their thoughts, words and actions. Naturally, they are attracted to all things beautiful themselves, and will often possess works of art and numerous items of colorful clothing. Nature and the great outdoors also attract the attention of gentle Deer people.

Deer people are also skillful with language, and use their quick minds and intuition. They possess the 'gift of the gab,' and appear quite jovial and witty when in the company of others. Many Deer people are often termed 'socialites.'

Deer just love company, and they are energized when around others, far more so than when they are on their own. Given their active type of energy, Deer people like to be kept busy and entertained.

Deer people are colorful and entertaining to others, and very accepting of other people's viewpoints and situations. Deer people have no interest in changing other people: their focus is on being socially desirable themselves.

# THE WOODPECKER

**Season:** Early summer — a time of long, hot days
**Season totem:** Coyote
**Season element:** Water
**Birth time:** 6/21–7/22 northern hemisphere
12/22–1/19 southern hemisphere
**Birth time element:** Water
**Elemental clan:** Frog
**Energy flow:** Receptive
**Affinities:** Color: pink
            Plant: wild rose
            Mineral: carnelian

**Gifts:** Intuition, loving nature, generosity, sensitivity, trust, devotion, loyalty, calmness
**Challenges:** Vulnerability, insecurity, gullibility, anxiety
**Life path:** To take time out each day to love and nurture yourself as much as you do others, and to stay true to yourself and what you feel is right.

## WOODPECKER PEOPLE

Woodpeckers are respected by Native Americans for their unique drumming behavior, as this is seen to represent the beating of the heart. Hearing a Woodpecker play its song out loud to the world is a sign to Native Americans to tune into their own heart song and courageously follow its message.

Woodpecker people live their lives according to what they feel is right. They listen to their hearts rather than their minds, thus avoiding an overly logical approach to decision-making.

Woodpeckers are seen as the most nurturing, charitable and generous of all people. They are blessed with naturally strong principles and values, to which they adhere in their everyday lives. They have an open mind about everyone they meet, and an open heart for all. They are neither discriminatory nor distrusting.

To Woodpeckers, the whole world is just one large extended family. They are particularly home-oriented. They value their relationships with others highly. As family and friends mean a lot to Woodpeckers, they take their commitments seriously, generously opening their homes and giving of themselves and what they possess to ease the hardships of others. Woodpeckers thrive when in the company of others.

With all of these qualities, Woodpeckers are quite naturally intuitive, and sensitive to their environment and those around them. They are particularly good in a crisis, when their calm and caring approach is much appreciated.

# THE SALMON

**Season:** Heart of summer — a time of ripening, of reaching growth potential
**Season totem:** Coyote
**Season element:** Water
**Birth time:** 7/23–8/22 northern hemisphere
1/20–2/18 southern hemisphere
**Birth time element:** Fire
**Elemental clan:** Thunderbird
**Energy flow:** Active
**Affinities:** Color: red
           Plant: raspberry
           Mineral: garnet

**Gifts:** Energy, versatility, sensuality, benevolence, determination, affection, charm, courage
**Challenges:** Impulsiveness, arrogance, selfishness, greed
**Life path:** To harness the vital energies that can surge through you, in order to achieve emotional balance and harmony with your environment.

## SALMON PEOPLE

In the wild, Salmon are required to swim back upstream, against the rushing tide, to find their spawning grounds. American Indians respect them for their vital energy and determination. Sighting Salmon on their trek upstream is a reminder to us to take stock of our own vital energies to ensure they are kept in control and directed positively.

Salmon people are out-going, action-oriented people who find it difficult to slow their hectic daily pace. They are robust, and usually look larger than life. Gregarious and versatile, they are bombastic when communicating. At the very least, Salmon people always stand out in a crowd.

At their best, Salmon people appear friendly and charming, never failing to entertain in social settings. At their worst, they can be erratic, even impulsive, and hot tempered and almost vengeful if they allow their emotions to run unchecked.

When the situation calls for courage, Salmon people are usually first in line. This makes them naturally suited to leadership roles, where their big-hearted and magnanimous approach to others can be widely appreciated.

Salmon people are also sensually active. They take pride in their appearance, and even more in their sexual prowess. They sometimes need to curb their personal desires in order to ensure that selfishness and greed do not take control of their actions, and in the process misdirect their honor and integrity.

# THE BROWN BEAR

**Season:** Late summer — harvesting time, a time to reap what has been sown
**Season totem:** Coyote
**Season element:** Water
**Birth time:** 8/23–9/22 northern hemisphere
2/19–3/20 southern hemisphere
**Birth time element:** Earth
**Elemental clan:** Turtle
**Energy flow:** Receptive
**Affinities:** Color: purple
　　　　　Plant: violet
　　　　　Mineral: amethyst

**Gifts:** Perseverance, judgment, fairness and justice, powers of discrimination, responsibility, commonsense, courage, wisdom
**Challenges:** Cynicism, critical nature, aloofness, conventionalism
**Life path:** To provide space in your life to nurture the spiritual core and in the process achieve the ultimate — balance between the physical, emotional and spiritual planes.

## Brown Bear People

The sheer size and strength of Brown Bears provides them with much magnetism and presence. American Indians have due respect for the Brown Bear, admiring its hunting skills and the strong protection it gives its young.

Brown Bear people at their best are hard-working, discerning and tenacious. They often demonstrate good judgment in their decision-making, and fairness and consideration when dealing with others. Where there is a problem, when someone is in distress or even when something is broken, Brown Bear people feel it their responsibility to fix it all. In fact, they may have the talent of being able to fix just about anything.

Like their animal totem, Brown Bear people have a strong physical presence. They attract the attention of others by their courage at standing up for what they believe is fair and just, and make protective and loyal friends, family members and work colleagues.

Their particular gifts lie in their considered approach to life and their perseverance. They are realistic, practical, analytical and deliberate people who demonstrate good sense and self–reliance. Brown Bear people can rise to meet any challenge life throws at them. Seeing a Brown Bear person triumph through a difficult time is a pure vision of perseverance in action.

While they are at their best in the physical world, Brown Bear people also have a natural tie to the world of the heart and their emotions. So, as well as being physically magnificent, Brown Bear people are at the same time gentle, warm, caring, cheerful and good-natured.

# THE RAVEN

**Season:** Early autumn — a time of browning and falling leaves, shortening days

**Season totem:** Grizzly Bear

**Season element:** Earth

**Birth time:** 9/23–10/22 northern hemisphere

3/21–4/19 southern hemisphere

**Birth time element:** Air

**Elemental clan:** Butterfly

**Energy flow:** Active

**Affinities:** Color: brown

Plant: mullein

Mineral: bloodstone jasper

**Gifts:** Intelligence, insight, intuition, inspiration, diplomacy, influence, adaptability, resourcefulness

**Challenges:** Depression, indecision, confusion, manipulativeness

**Life path:** To explore and comprehend humans' inner darkness, and then to act as the communication medium between the physical and spiritual worlds for others.

## RAVEN PEOPLE

Ravens, as black as night itself, are said by American Indians to possess magical powers. Their medicine is rather strong: sighting one is a message to turn and face your inner darkness and your fears, and transform your life.

Raven people are extraordinarily special individuals, as they act as natural catalysts for the transformation of other people's lives. To achieve this, they are especially intuitive and diplomatic, demonstrating great care and consideration for their fellow humans. They are generally open-hearted, charming and peace-loving people who demonstrate exceptional communication skills, particularly in terms of listening.

Ravens have a strong social conscience, which can lead them to be overly idealistic at times. As they are good at starting things, you will often find them working tirelessly behind the scenes to influence those in power, getting them to restore and maintain harmony and peace within their communities.

Raven people tend to dislike solitude, preferring the company of others, whether in a social, business or personal context. Physically attractive and affectionate, they need to give and receive physical affection regularly, otherwise they could slip into a depressive or confused emotional state that would all too easily disrupt their harmonious natures.

At their best, Raven people are quite in tune with their physical and emotional sides. This leaves only one real challenge — to develop their latent psychic abilities. If they do so, they could be of much greater service to others, as healers or as psychic mediums.

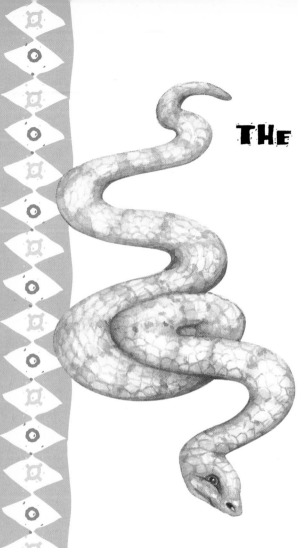

# THE SNAKE

**Season:** The heart of autumn — a time of early morning frosts and the coming of the cold
**Season totem:** Grizzly Bear
**Season element:** Earth
**Birth time:** 10/23–11/21 northern hemisphere
4/20–5/20 southern hemisphere
**Birth time element:** Water
**Elemental clan:** Frog
**Energy flow:** Receptive
**Affinities:** Color: orange
Plant: thistle
Mineral: copper

**Gifts:** Patience, sensuality, ambition, charisma, wisdom, detachment, imagination, vitality
**Challenges:** Jealousy, deceitfulness, stubbornness, critical nature
**Life path:** To take a dose of your own medicine regularly: to stop resisting changing yourself, and to go within regularly to experience your own animal totem power of transformation.

## SNAKE PEOPLE

Snakes represent many things to American Indians. First, they are seen as the ultimate transformative creatures, given their ability to shed their skins to suit their environments — this also demonstrates their superior survival skills. In addition, Snakes are prized for their sensual, hypnotic influence, and are therefore often associated with physical desirability and procreation.

Snake people are said to have survived many trials in previous lives and, accordingly, to have earned the right to be linked to this auspicious animal totem. To have survived a snakebite is a sign of having passed a physical and/or spiritual test. Therefore, Snake people are hardy, physically and mentally strong, and durable. They are life's real survivors, and can regenerate quickly after setbacks.

Their keen observation skills and sensory acuity provide Snake people with insights into other people and environments that few can match. Snake people are the most skilled catalysts of change in others and in external events. However, this also means that Snake people are more resistant to changing themselves. They are determined and patient, and have intense self-control.

Snake people do tend to have highly charged sex drives, often hinted at by their physical intensity, smoldering sensuality and striking good looks. For Snake people to meet their sensual needs and fulfill their desires requires much of their significant reserve of physical and emotional energy.

Snake people are ambitious, usually acquiring success and wealth easily. They are driven to accumulate things such as money and possessions, but also like to accumulate new people and life experiences.

# THE OWL

**Season:** Late autumn — a time of long nights and the arrival of the first snows
**Season totem:** Grizzly Bear
**Season element:** Earth
**Birth time:** 11/22–12/21 northern hemisphere
5/21–6/20 southern hemisphere
**Birth time element:** Fire
**Elemental clan:** Thunderbird
**Energy flow:** Active
**Affinities:** Color: black
      Plant: black spruce pine
      Mineral: obsidian — volcanic glass/granite

**Gifts:** Self-reliance, expressiveness, inquisitiveness, wisdom, justice, sense, intelligence, discretion
**Challenges:** Conventionalism, intolerance, pride, dominance
**Life path:** To cultivate and practice tolerance in your everyday dealings with others, especially those less gifted and developed than you.

# OWL PEOPLE

The Owl is frequently referred to by American Indians as the night eagle or the night's friend. A large bird of prey with a distinctive cry, it has huge eyes that give it the power to see through the darkest of nights. Native Americans believe the Owl can see and know everything. Sighting one in the wild is a sign that you should become more observant of what can't be seen at a physical level, or that it is time for you to face your darkest fears.

Owl people are intelligent, very observant, and sensible. While young Owls are growing up they may be described as 'wise beyond their years,' and wisdom is a gift they carry throughout their lives. Owl people have an inner strength, an ability to be both soft and strong in their personalities.

Given their eye for detail and their almost clairvoyant ability to read the thoughts and intentions of others, Owl people are very difficult to deceive. They can get to the heart of any matter in record time, leaving others still confused about how they did it, and frustrated in any plan to put one over the wise, all-knowing Owl.

The only risks Owl people take in life are those they have calculated thoroughly. Hence, they rarely make a poor decision or take an incorrect action. Regret is an emotion Owls just don't get to experience.

It's not surprising, then, that in modern society, judges or school principals are often represented as owls. Owl people have strong ethics and principles, and a clear sense of fairness and justice. In addition, they like to be in positions of power — ideally those that will allow them to make decisions about right or wrong, guilt or innocence — and then dispense any punishment due.

# INFLUENCE OF THE ELEMENTS AND THE SEASONS

# THE ELEMENTS OF NATURE

In the American Indian belief system, fire, water, air and earth are the four elements that act as nature's forces. The four interact to ensure that living things go through a recurring process of birth, life, death and regeneration. In animal totem astrology, the four distinct seasons are each governed by an element, as is each of the twelve birth times and their corresponding birth totems.

This means that each animal totem has two particular elements influencing its character and behavior at any one time. If we take the two elements and their key attributes into account when analyzing each animal totem's character, we will gain a more detailed and accurate description of that totem.

| Element | Key attributes | Areas governed by the element |
|---------|----------------|-------------------------------|
| Fire | Energy, passion, decisiveness, illumination, expansion | The spirit & intuition |
| Water | Sensitivity, flexibility, intuition, creativity, communication | The soul & emotions |
| Earth | Stability, balance, patience, practicality, realism | The physical body & physical sensations |
| Air | Communication, intelligence, renewal, thought, logic | The mind & psyche |

The following sections will help you to find your season and birth time elements. Once you know what these elements are and how they affect your personality, return to this page to study what additional attributes are at work in your personality.

# SEASON ELEMENTS

Just as there are recurring seasons in nature, so there are seasons to life in general. The following table shows the link between the seasons, their elements, time of life and the twelve birth totems.

| Season | Direction on Medicine Wheel | Time of day it governs |
|--------|------------------------------|------------------------|
| Spring | East | Sunrise to morning |
| Summer | South | Midday |
| Autumn | West | Afternoon to sunset |
| Winter | North | Night |

Each element governing a season of birth brings special qualities to the three animal totems for that season. These qualities relate to the totems' inner senses, spiritual endeavors and general behavior.

## SPRING ANIMAL TOTEMS

The spring animal totems Hawk, Beaver and Deer have the force of fire directing their general behavior. Hence, people born during this season generally act with great energy, passion and decisiveness. They have spirited natures, and, generally, well-developed intuition.

## Summer animal totems

The summer animal totems, Woodpecker, Salmon and Brown Bear, have the force of water directing their general behavior. People born during this time of the year therefore tend to act with sensitivity toward others. They have flexible and creative natures, and their communication skills are generally well developed.

| Time of life it governs | Animal birth totem | Season element |
|---|---|---|
| Birth & youth (0–18 years) | Hawk, Beaver, Deer | Fire |
| Adulthood (18–40 years) | Woodpecker, Salmon, Brown Bear | Water |
| Middle life (40–60 years) | Raven, Snake, Owl | Earth |
| Old age (60+) | Snow Goose, Otter, Wolf | Air |

## Autumn animal totems

The autumn animal totems, Raven, Snake and Owl, have the force of earth directing their general behavior. Hence people born during this time generally act with patience and a great deal of realism. They have balanced and stable natures and are quite practical.

## Winter animal totems

The winter animal totems, Snow Goose, Otter and Wolf, have the force of air directing their behavior. People born during this time usually show good verbal expression and logic. They have thoughtful and reflective natures and are quite intelligent.

## Birth Time Elements

The element ruling each birth time influences on the instinctive behavior of each animal totem. It is this element that creates the foundation of each animal totem's basic nature — the essence of who you are. You will see from the examples below that the different elements cause differences in personality, highlighting particular strengths and weaknesses of character. As a result, people with different birth time elements will often have complementary natures. This reflects the American Indian philosophy that we are all part of a spiritual whole, and rely on others for completeness. Just as the four elements depend on one other for their existence, so do the people of the earth.

Each of the four elements is linked with three of the twelve birth-time animal totems. The birth time elements are given below, followed by brief notes on the aspects of character shared by animal totems with the same birth time element.

| Animal totem | Birth time element |
|---|---|
| Snow Goose | Earth |
| Otter | Air |
| Wolf | Water |
| Hawk | Fire |
| Beaver | Earth |
| Deer | Air |
| Woodpecker | Water |
| Salmon | Fire |
| Brown Bear | Earth |
| Raven | Air |
| Snake | Water |
| Owl | Fire |

Snow Goose, Beaver and Brown Bear: EARTH
With earth as their birth time element, these animal totems all have patience and practicality at the core of their natures. They tend to operate by using their well-developed common sense. They are realistic and emotionally balanced.

Otter, Deer and Raven: AIR
With air as their birth time element, these animal totems all have keen intellects and inquiring minds. Otter, Deer and Raven people tend to operate using logic and rational thought. They are clever individuals, with psychic abilities.

Wolf, Woodpecker and Snake: WATER
With water as their birth time element, these animal totems are emotionally sensitive and flexible. They operate by using their usually well-developed intuition and communication skills. They are empathetic and creative.

Hawk, Salmon and Owl: FIRE
With fire as their birth time element, these animal totems are passionate and enthusiastic to the very core of their beings. They tend to operate very energetically and decisively. They are go-getters, and tend to thrive on change.

## PURE SIGNS

Pure signs occur when the season and birth time elements are the same. In animal totem astrology, three animal totems are pure signs. These are:

• Otter — Air of Air

• Hawk — Fire of Fire

• Woodpecker — Water of Water

People with these totems express the attributes of their elements intensely.

### OTTER PEOPLE

People of the Otter totem reflect the attributes of air more than any other animal totem. This means their minds are acutely developed, they are highly intelligent, and they have particularly strong psychic powers.

With such attributes, Otter people are challenged more than any other sign to seek balance regularly with the earth, to ensure they remain practical and grounded in their everyday lives.

### HAWK PEOPLE

People of the Hawk totem demonstrate a great capacity for growth and expansion. They are highly energized, extremely passionate and spirited individuals.

With such highly developed physical energies, Hawk people are challenged more than any other sign to keep under control the fires that can burn so fiercely inside them. This means tempering their emotional responses and balancing their vital energies. In particular, they need to take their time, considering the likely consequences of their actions and words before diving in.

### WOODPECKER PEOPLE

People of the Woodpecker totem demonstrate highly refined intuition and creativity. With their very flexible and intuitive natures, they are the supreme communicators.

With so much flexibility and creativity, Woodpecker people, more than any other sign, need to take a stand on their personal convictions and principles. They should learn to take decisive action to realize their ideas. They also need to approach their everyday activities in a methodical fashion, so these activities can bear fruit for the benefit of all.

# Season Totems

In the American Indian astrology system, people have season totems as well as birth totems. The season totems give us additional gifts and qualities.

## Springtime Animal Totem: The Eagle
*Direction:* East    *Element:* Fire

Eagles are awesome birds of prey, with tremendous strength and vitality, along with the ability to fly extremely high and far in search of prey. This is believed to give them vision, and clarity about both the present and the future. Eagles are believed by Native Americans to be messengers for The Creator of the World, bringing enlightenment to the people of the earth.

People born during spring — Hawk people, Beaver people and Deer people — all have the Eagle as their season totem. They are all filled with youthful vitality, and have a natural interest in personal growth and development. They tend to be early risers, as they want to greet the dawn of each new day — this is the time of day they are at their most productive. They represent the human lifetime of childhood and adolescence, from birth to approximately age 18.

**Additional gifts Eagle bestows on Hawk, Beaver and Deer**
- Passion, enthusiasm and optimism
- Energy in abundance for physical activity
- Clarity about present circumstances
- Vision of future possibilities

**The lessons Eagle brings to Hawk, Beaver and Deer**
- the need to temper their passion and enthusiasm so they don't overwhelm others
- the need to control their energy so that it is not dissipated, but used for worthwhile causes instead

## SUMMERTIME ANIMAL TOTEM: THE COYOTE

*Direction:* South     *Element:* Water

Coyotes are wild and wily animals who have so far proved adaptable to the encroachment of civilization on their natural terrain. They use their agility and sharp senses to avoid unnecessary contact with humans.

People born during summer — Woodpecker people, Salmon people and Brown Bear people — all have the Coyote as their season totem. They often experience rapid growth, either physically, mentally, emotionally or spiritually. They are most productive in the heat of the day — at midday — when their sharp senses can be utilized and their newly developed maturity well tested. They represent the human lifetime of young adulthood, from approximately 18 to 40 years of age.

**Additional gifts Coyote bestows on Woodpecker, Salmon and Brown Bear**
- Swiftness of body and mind
- Sensory acuity
- Independence
- Self-reliance

**The lessons Coyote brings to Woodpecker, Salmon and Brown Bear**
- the need to go in search of what feels right in order to find their calling
- the need to experience and trust in life in order to grow

## AUTUMNTIME ANIMAL TOTEM: THE GRIZZLY BEAR

*Direction:* West     *Element:* Earth

Grizzly Bears are enormous and powerful creatures, who lead calm and mostly peaceful lives. They are slow moving, but every move is one of determination and confidence. Their hibernation is believed by Native Americans to demonstrate their obvious capacity for introspection, renewal and the gaining of wisdom.

People born during the autumn — Raven people, Snake people and Owl people — all have the Grizzly Bear as their season totem. Raven, Snake and Owl people all have the capability and wisdom to hold powerful and responsible positions within the community, such as those of the leader, healer or teacher. They are calm and confident in any situation. They enjoy twilight — late afternoon — a time when they can reflect on and appraise what they have achieved throughout the day. They represent the human lifetime of mid-life, from approximately 40 to 60 years of age.

**Additional gifts Grizzly Bear bestows on Raven, Snake and Owl**
- introspection and understanding of their own hearts
- confidence and wisdom in any given situation
- the desire to assume responsibility for their own words and actions
- the strength to be accountable for their words and actions

**The lessons Grizzly Bear brings to Raven, Snake and Owl**
- the need to acknowledge both their strengths and their weaknesses
- the need to have a strong yet calm and controlled center, from which power will issue

## WINTERTIME ANIMAL TOTEM: THE WHITE BUFFALO

*Direction:* North     *Element:* Air

The White Buffalo was a rare animal, sacred to Native Americans. It would sacrifice itself totally for the well-being of humans. Its meat, hide, horns and other parts were all utilized by the tribe for everything from food and clothing to shelter and weapons. The Buffalo was believed to be the messenger of knowledge, an animal holding a spiritual union with The Creator of the World.

People born during winter — Snow Goose people, Otter people and Wolf people — all have the White Buffalo as their season totem. They are wise, independent and people-oriented. They are highly intelligent and have active minds. As they like to take time out to rejuvenate, their best time is the night. Sleep brings them rest, and their dreams bring them powerful messages and lessons on life. They represent the human lifetime of old age, from around age 60 onward.

**Additional gifts White Buffalo bestows on Snow Goose, Otter and Wolf**
- Intelligence and wisdom
- Self-sacrifice and charity
- Spirituality
- Generosity

**The lessons White Buffalo brings to Snow Goose, Otter and Wolf**
- the need to rest and rejuvenate physically and emotionally in order to grow spiritually
- the need to keep contact with the earthly realm — to stay balanced and be realistic and practical

# Elemental Clans

Your elemental clan is the animal group you belong to as determined by your birth time element.

## Thunderbird clan: Fire totems — Hawk, Salmon, Owl

 The Thunderbird, the largest and most magnificent of the Hawks, is now extinct, living in spirit only. An American Indian myth tells how the Thunderbird fell prey to arrogance, developing an inflated ego. In a burst of fire from a thunderbolt sent by The Creator, it was raised from the earth to become a spirit.

Like their elemental animal totem, Hawk, Salmon and Owl people are powerful, radiant and passionate. They have spirited and enthusiastic personalities, and thriving on activity and change. They are charming and witty people who love being the center of attention, delighting in acknowledgment and praise from others.

Just like fire, their emotions can vary in the extreme, from warm to blazing. The deeper and more developed their maturity and control of their emotions, the less likely they are to be overwhelming to others.

**Strengths to cultivate:** Intuition, physical stamina, optimism, motivation

**Possible weaknesses to address:** Gullibility to flattery, inflated ego, oversensitivity to constructive criticism

## Frog clan: Water totems — Wolf, Woodpecker, Snake

The Frog is a very distinctive and adaptable creature. Its body is slick and nimble, and this gives it much agility and flexibility. Its signature 'croak' is a serenade to many, and the metamorphosis from tadpole to adult frog demonstrates its ability to transform itself.

Like their elemental animal totem, Wolf, Woodpecker and Snake people are very flexible and emotionally fluid individuals who possess the ability to transform themselves to suit their environments. The water element provides them with creativity and expressiveness, making them skilled communicators.

Just like water, Frog clan members' creativity can shift from stagnant pools and dams to rushing tides and pounding waves. Their ideas and innovations have the capacity to transform people and environments, provided they can set clear directions and apply the discipline required for reaching their goals.

**Strengths to cultivate:** Empathy, communication, creativity, emotional accessibility

**Possible weaknesses to address:** Repression of emotions, stagnation of ideas, lack of discipline, inability to change emotional responses

## Turtle clan: Earth totems — Snow Goose, Beaver, Brown Bear

 The Turtle is one of the oldest surviving animals on earth today. It is also one of the most harmonious. Its ability to use the earth and sun for laying its eggs and hatching its young while it lives predominantly in the water demonstrates the balance it has achieved among the elements.

Like their element and their elemental animal totem, Snow Goose, Beaver and Brown Bear people are grounded, stable and secure. They are loyal, and act according to their strong values and principles. They are very practical, constructive and industrious.

Just like their element, they can be nurturing and sustaining to those around them — but this all depends on the generosity of their soul. They will only be of value to themselves and others if they learn to accommodate the qualities of all the other elements — fire, air and water.

**Strengths to cultivate:** Responsibility and accountability, self-sacrifice, being sensible, diligence

**Possible weaknesses to address:** Stubbornness, authoritative approach when dealing with others, intolerance to others' views and beliefs

## BUTTERFLY CLAN: AIR TOTEMS — OTTER, DEER, RAVEN

 Butterflies are colorful, graceful and weightless. They begin life as caterpillars, only to be transformed into their beautiful and free flowing state after an intense metamorphosis while wrapped in a silky, soft and protective cocoon. To the American Indians, they are a symbol of change, transformation and hope.

Like their elemental animal totem, Otter, Deer and Raven people are beautiful to behold and delightful to have around. They are active, energetic and ever-changing, in physical appearance as well as in their feelings, thoughts and opinions. As such, they have the power to transform and uplift those around them. They are intelligent, innovative and expressive individuals.

But their appearance and behavior can be most deceiving, even to themselves. Just like the element of air, Butterfly clan members can appear to float on anything — from a mere breath of fresh air to hurricane-force winds. If they are nurtured and respected, they will remain calm and refreshing. If they are angered, they may quickly erupt into an overpowering fury.

**Strengths to cultivate:** Flexibility, spirituality, optimism, humanitarianism

**Possible weaknesses to address:** Lack of practicality and perseverance, lack of control in emotional responses

# ANIMAL TOTEM PAIRINGS – RELATIONSHIP STRENGTHS AND CHALLENGES

Now that you have an in-depth knowledge of the different animal totems, you may be wondering how compatible the various animal totems are with one another. This section presents relationship strengths and potential challenges for all possible animal pairings.

# CONTENTS

# THE SNOW GOOSE

## Ideal pairings

| Snow Goose & | Relationship potential |
| --- | --- |
| Beaver | Both are hardworking and practical-minded, and hence each will respect the other's loyalty and dedication throughout life. |
| Brown Bear | Both are dedicated and methodical individuals who will provide each other with the support and encouragement they desire for their endeavors. |
| Wolf | Snow Goose will be encouraged to develop spirituality through this association, and Wolf will be provided with direction and determination. |
| Snake | Sensuous Snake will ignite Snow Goose's primal energies. Snow Goose will keep all Snake's wavering principles and values in check. |
| Woodpecker | **Complement.** A natural attraction and kinship exists between these two animal totems. Each will make the other a loyal and supportive companion. |

## Challenging pairings

| Snow Goose & | Relationship potential |
| --- | --- |
| Otter | Both have air as their season element, which means they have similar lessons to learn in life. They can help each other — provided both are mature enough to respect their differences. |
| Hawk | Snow Goose will grow increasingly frustrated with Hawk's impatience. Hawk will find Snow Goose too stubborn and unwilling to change. |
| Deer | Snow Goose will find Deer superficial, and Deer will soon be dismissed. Deer will be too easily hurt by Snow Goose's arrogance. |
| Salmon | Both have extremely healthy egos, making it difficult for either to compromise. |
| Raven | Serious and authoritative Snow Goose will not be able to lift Raven's occasional depression. Snow Goose will see no value in the union. |
| Owl | Both will want to dominate the relationship, and antagonism will build over time. |
| Snow Goose | Snow Goose pairing with another will bring about a mirroring effect, whereby the best and the worst in each other will be magnified. |

# THE OTTER

**Ideal pairings**

| Otter & | Relationship potential |
| --- | --- |
| Deer | This pair has the potential for a fun-filled and harmonious life together. There is little capacity for friction in either. |
| Raven | Both have strong humanitarian values and will find in each other the support and encouragement they require. |
| Hawk | Both are quite active and optimistic individuals. Their energies will easily match, and each will strengthen the other. |
| Owl | This pair will make a good match. Owl will provide wisdom and the sensible touch, while Otter will provide Owl with youthful enthusiasm. |
| Salmon | **Complement.** Each will make a loyal and supportive companion to the other. A natural attraction and kinship exists between these two animal totems. |

**Challenging pairings**

| Otter & | Relationship potential |
| --- | --- |
| Snow Goose | Both have air as their season element, so they have similar lessons to learn in life. They can help each other — provided both are mature enough to respect their differences. |
| Wolf | Otter will fruitlessly endeavor to raise Wolf from melancholy states, while Wolf will fail to provide the support Otter requires for achieving goals. |
| Beaver | They live on opposite sides of the stream. Beaver is industrious, and prefers to work. Otter is imaginative, and prefers to play. |
| Woodpecker | Both lack drive and ambition, hence neither will be able to help the other in productive endeavors. |
| Brown Bear | Otters are optimistic daredevils, while Brown Bears are cynical and far too serious. Neither can meet the other's expectations. |
| Snake | Snake will constantly be jealous of Otter's popularity and will soon seek the limelight with other, less attractive companions. |
| Otter | An Otter pairing with another will bring about a mirroring effect, whereby the best and the worst in each other will be magnified. |

# THE WOLF

## Ideal pairings

| Wolf & | Relationship potential |
| --- | --- |
| Woodpecker | Given their emotion-centered approach to life, each will be sensitive, and loyal to the other. |
| Snake | Wolf will be happy to let Snake take control in the relationship and will be thankful for Snake's wise counsel. Snake will be content with Wolf's selflessness. |
| Snow Goose | Snow Goose will be encouraged to develop spirituality through this association, and Wolf will be provided with direction and determination. |
| Beaver | Wolf will gain materialistically from a union with the industrious Beaver. Beaver will admire Wolf's philosophical and spiritual approach to life. |
| Brown Bear | **Complement.** A natural attraction and kinship exists between these two animal totems. Each will make the other a loyal and supportive companion. |

## Challenging pairings

| Wolf & | Relationship potential |
| --- | --- |
| Otter | Otter will fruitlessly endeavor to raise Wolf from melancholy states, while Wolf will fail to provide the support Otter requires for achieving goals. |
| Hawk | Hawk is impatient and impulsive, while Wolf is restless and indecisive. Neither will be able to make a decision that will make both happy. |
| Deer | Both can be extremely nervous types. They may experience high anxiety while in a relationship together. |
| Salmon | Salmon is likely to take advantage of Wolf's trusting heart. Wolf will soon leave the relationship wounded and depressed. |
| Raven | As neither are capable of making decisions in a relationship, nothing will be achieved. This could open the door to depression for both. |
| Owl | Owl will be frustrated, and intolerant of Wolf's indecisiveness and sensitivity. Wolf will soon feel it better to go it alone. |
| Wolf | Wolf pairing with another will bring about a mirroring effect, whereby the best and the worst in each other will be magnified. |

# THE HAWK

## Ideal pairings

| Hawk & | Relationship potential |
| --- | --- |
| Salmon | Both have high energy. Hawk will provide the ideas and foresight, while Salmon will provide the determination necessary for enacting all plans. |
| Owl | Both have a strong sense of right and wrong. They will find their values match, and will be happy to live according to their principles and ethics. |
| Otter | Both are quite active and optimistic individuals. Their energies will easily match, and each will strengthen the other. |
| Deer | Hawk will provide Deer with boldness and foresight, while Deer will encourage Hawk's gentler side. |
| Raven | **Complement.** A natural attraction and kinship exists between these two animal totems. Each will make the other a loyal and supportive companion. |

## Challenging pairings

| Hawk & | Relationship potential |
| --- | --- |
| Snow Goose | Snow Goose will grow increasingly frustrated with Hawk's impatience. Hawk will find Snow Goose too stubborn and unwilling to change. |
| Beaver | Steadfast Beaver will come into the relationship with set opinions. Hawk will want to take a more liberal approach. They will soon part. |
| Woodpecker | These two operate at different levels. Hawks are bold and independent, while Woodpeckers are introverted and dependent. Neither will have their needs met in this relationship. |
| Brown Bear | Impulsive Hawk will find the methodical Brown Bear stodgy and stifling. Brown Bear will soon be openly criticizing Hawk's impulsive behavior. |
| Snake | Snake is patient, while Hawk is rash. Neither will be able to understand the other's behavior. They will soon depart to find more compatible companions. |
| Wolf | Hawk is impatient and impulsive, while Wolf is restless and indecisive. Neither will be able to make a decision that will make both happy. |
| Hawk | Hawk pairing with another will bring about a mirroring effect, whereby the best and the worst in each other will be magnified. |

# The Beaver

## Ideal pairings

| Beaver & | Relationship potential |
| --- | --- |
| Brown Bear | Both are industrious and reliable. Much can be accomplished and accumulated when Beaver and Brown Bear get together. |
| Snow Goose | Both are hardworking and practical-minded; hence, each will respect the other's loyalty and dedication throughout life. |
| Wolf | Wolf will gain materialistically from a union with the industrious Beaver. Beaver will admire Wolf's philosophical and spiritual approach to life. |
| Woodpecker | Woodpecker's loving nature and devotion will be enough to soften the usually inflexible nature of Beaver, who will reward Woodpecker with material security. |
| Snake | **Complement.** A natural attraction and kinship exists between these two animal totems. Each will make the other a loyal and supportive companion. |

## Challenging pairings

| Beaver & | Relationship potential |
| --- | --- |
| Otter | They live on opposite sides of the stream. Beaver is industrious, and prefers to work. Otter is imaginative, and prefers to play. |
| Hawk | Steadfast Beaver will come into the relationship with set opinions. Hawk will want to take a more liberal approach. They will soon part. |
| Deer | Deer will prove too sensitive and coy for the tenacious and opinionated Beaver. Beaver and Deer are rarely attracted to each other — their natures are worlds apart. |
| Salmon | Salmon will want excitement and sensual stimulation from Beaver, and Beaver will want practicality and endeavor. Both will end up empty-handed. |
| Raven | Influential Raven achieves success through others, while Beaver achieves success through sheer hard work. There will be no appreciation for each other's tactics. |
| Owl | Each will want to dominate the other in this relationship. Beaver will remain inflexible despite Owl's attempts to exert influence, and Owl will be too proud to give Beaver any ground. |
| Beaver | Beaver pairing with another will bring about a mirroring effect, whereby the best and the worst in each other will be magnified. |

# THE DEER

## Ideal pairings

| Deer & | Relationship potential |
| --- | --- |
| Otter | This pair has the potential for a fun-filled and harmonious life together. There is little capacity for friction in either. |
| Raven | This pair will exude grace and charm. They are both active, and will be quite communicative with one another. |
| Hawk | Hawk will provide Deer with boldness and foresight, while Deer will encourage Hawk's gentler side. |
| Salmon | Both are versatile, and this will be mutually attractive. Deer will be happy to be directed by the determined Salmon, who will bestow much affection on Deer. |
| Owl | **Complement.** A natural attraction and kinship exists between these two animal totems. Each will make the other a loyal and supportive companion. |

## Challenging pairings

| Deer & | Relationship potential |
| --- | --- |
| Wolf | Both can be extremely nervous types. They may experience high anxiety while in a relationship together. |
| Snow Goose | Snow Goose will find Deer superficial, and Deer will soon be dismissed. Deer will be too easily hurt by Snow Goose's arrogance. |
| Beaver | Deer will prove too sensitive and coy for the tenacious and opinionated Beaver. Beaver and Deer are rarely attracted to each other — their natures are worlds apart. |
| Woodpecker | Both are prone to nervousness and insecurity. Theirs would be a vulnerable relationship, lacking in any real support and practicality. |
| Brown Bear | Where Brown Bear will persevere, Deer will prefer to give in. When Deer is in need of affection, Brown Bear will be aloof. These two will have little in common. |
| Snake | Snake can take the hard knocks in life, while Deer has a tendency to falter. Snake will think Deer weak, and Deer will think Snake too rigid and critical. |
| Deer | Deer pairing with another will bring about a mirroring effect, whereby the best and the worst in each other will be magnified. |

# THE WOODPECKER

## Ideal pairings

| Woodpecker & | Relationship potential |
|---|---|
| Snake | The relationship will be sensuous and mutually satisfying. Both Snake and Woodpecker have significant emotional needs that the other can meet. |
| Wolf | Given their emotion-centered approach to life, each will be sensitive, and loyal to the other. |
| Beaver | Woodpecker's loving nature and devotion will be enough to soften the usually inflexible nature of Beaver, who will reward Woodpecker with material security. |
| Brown Bear | There will be an immediate attraction — Brown Bear will be unable to resist Woodpecker's generous and loyal nature, and Woodpecker will enjoy Brown Bear's courage and perseverance. |
| Snow Goose | **Complement.** A natural attraction and kinship exists between these two animal totems. Each will make the other a loyal and supportive companion. |

## Challenging pairings

| Woodpecker & | Relationship potential |
|---|---|
| Otter | Both lack drive and ambition, hence neither will be able to help the other in productive endeavors. |
| Hawk | These two operate at different levels. Hawks are bold and independent, while Woodpeckers are introverted and dependent. Neither will have their needs met in this relationship. |
| Deer | Both are prone to nervousness and insecurity. Theirs would be a vulnerable relationship, lacking in any real support and practicality. |
| Salmon | Woodpeckers like to stay at home and cuddle, while Salmon would rather go out and party. Each will go their own way in time. |
| Raven | Woodpecker will be too sensitive, and vulnerable to Raven's confusion and indecision. Raven will find Woodpecker lacking in energy and inspiration. |
| Owl | Owl is too self-reliant for Woodpecker to feel any true union between them. Owl will not find Woodpecker stimulating company. |
| Woodpecker | Woodpecker pairing with another will bring about a mirroring effect, whereby the best and the worst in each other will be magnified. |

# The Salmon

## Ideal pairings

| Salmon & | Relationship potential |
| --- | --- |
| Owl | Both have energy to burn, and will find the other stimulating company. Salmon can gain wise counsel from Owl, while Owl will find Salmon has an exciting charm. |
| Hawk | Both have high energy. Hawk will provide the ideas and foresight, while Salmon will provide the determination necessary for enacting all plans. |
| Deer | Both are versatile, and this will be mutually attractive. Deer will be happy to be directed by the determined Salmon, who will bestow much affection on Deer. |
| Raven | Intuitive Raven will supply energetic Salmon with clear direction. Salmon will provide Raven with the determination and courage needed for pursuing goals. |
| Otter | **Complement.** A natural attraction and kinship exists between these two animal totems. Each will make the other a loyal and supportive companion. |

## Challenging pairings

| Salmon & | Relationship potential |
| --- | --- |
| Snow Goose | Both have extremely healthy egos, and this will make it difficult for either to compromise. |
| Wolf | Salmon is likely to take advantage of wolf's trusting heart. Wolf will soon leave the relationship wounded and depressed. |
| Beaver | Salmon will want excitement and sensual stimulation from Beaver, and Beaver will want practicality and endeavor. Both will end up empty-handed. |
| Woodpecker | Woodpeckers like to stay at home and cuddle, while Salmon would rather go out and party. Each will go their own way in time. |
| Brown Bear | Cheerful Salmon will not be impressed with Brown Bear's cynicism, and Brown Bear will be too critical of Salmon's wayward charm and sensuality. |
| Snake | Both are quite sensual, but Salmon is openly affectionate, while Snake will only demonstrate feelings in private. Over time, they will come to feel uncomfortable in each other's company. |
| Salmon | Salmon pairing with another will bring about a mirroring effect, whereby the best and the worst in each other will be magnified. |

# THE BROWN BEAR

## Ideal pairings

| Brown Bear & | Relationship potential |
| --- | --- |
| Snow Goose | Both are dedicated and methodical individuals who will provide each other with the support and encouragement they desire for their endeavors. |
| Beaver | Both are industrious and reliable. Much can be accomplished and accumulated when Beaver and Brown Bear get together. |
| Woodpecker | There will be an immediate attraction — Brown Bear will be unable to resist Woodpecker's generous and loyal nature, and Woodpecker will enjoy Brown Bear's courage and perseverance. |
| Snake | Both are patient and wise individuals who will be able to see the numerous benefits in the relationship before physical attraction has even taken hold. |
| Wolf | **Complement.** A natural attraction and kinship exists between these two animal totems. Each will make the other a loyal and supportive companion. |

## Challenging pairings

| Brown Bear & | Relationship potential |
| --- | --- |
| Otter | Otters are optimistic daredevils, while Brown Bears are cynical and far too serious. Neither will meet the other's expectations. |
| Hawk | Impulsive Hawk will find the methodical Brown Bear stodgy and stifling. Brown Bear will soon be openly criticizing Hawk's impulsive behavior. |
| Deer | Where Brown Bear will persevere, Deer will prefer to give in. When Deer is in need of affection, Brown Bear will be aloof. These two will have little in common. |
| Salmon | Cheerful Salmon will not be impressed with Brown Bear's cynicism, and Brown Bear will be too critical of Salmon's wayward charm and sensuality. |
| Raven | Brown Bear will grow critical of Raven's idealistic goals and charitable inclinations. Raven will find Brown Bear lacking in enthusiasm. |
| Owl | These two opinionated and strong-willed individuals will clash on meeting. They will end up as adversaries in most situations. |
| Brown Bear | Brown Bear pairing with another will bring about a mirroring effect, whereby the best and the worst in each other will be magnified. |

# THE RAVEN

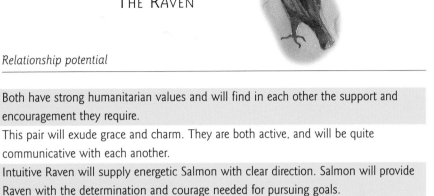

## Ideal pairings

| Raven & | Relationship potential |
| --- | --- |
| Otter | Both have strong humanitarian values and will find in each other the support and encouragement they require. |
| Deer | This pair will exude grace and charm. They are both active, and will be quite communicative with each another. |
| Salmon | Intuitive Raven will supply energetic Salmon with clear direction. Salmon will provide Raven with the determination and courage needed for pursuing goals. |
| Owl | Sensible Owl will encourage Raven's strong social conscience. Raven will reward Owl with influential networks and contacts. |
| Hawk | **Complement.** A natural attraction and kinship exists between these two animal totems. Each will make the other a loyal and supportive companion. |

## Challenging pairings

| Raven & | Relationship potential |
| --- | --- |
| Snow Goose | Serious and authoritative Snow Goose will not be able to lift Raven's occasional depression. Snow Goose will see no value in the union. |
| Wolf | As neither are capable of making decisions in a relationship, nothing will be achieved. This could open the door to depression for both. |
| Beaver | Influential Raven achieves success through others, while Beaver achieves success through sheer hard work. There will be no appreciation for each other's tactics. |
| Woodpecker | Woodpecker will be too sensitive, and vulnerable to Raven's confusion and indecision. Raven will find Woodpecker lacking in energy and inspiration. |
| Brown Bear | Brown Bear will grow critical of Raven's idealistic goals and charitable inclinations. Raven will find Brown Bear lacking in enthusiasm. |
| Snake | Raven will be open to manipulation and deception when Snake turns on the charisma. But Snake will soon tire of the game, and Raven will feel lucky to be out of the union. |
| Raven | Raven pairing with another will bring about a mirroring effect, whereby the best and the worst in each other will be magnified. |

# THE SNAKE

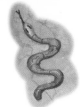

## Ideal pairings

| Snake & | Relationship potential |
|---|---|
| Wolf | Wolf will be happy to let Snake take control in the relationship and will be thankful for Snake's wise counsel. Snake will be content with Wolf's selflessness. |
| Woodpecker | The relationship will be sensuous and mutually satisfying. Both Snake and Woodpecker have significant emotional needs that the other can meet. |
| Snow Goose | Sensuous Snake will ignite Snow Goose's primal energies. Snow Goose will keep all Snake's wavering principles and values in check. |
| Brown Bear | Both are patient and wise individuals who will be able to see the numerous benefits in the relationship before physical attraction has even taken hold. |
| Beaver | **Complement.** A natural attraction and kinship exists between these two animal totems. Each will make the other a loyal and supportive companion. |

## Challenging pairings

| Snake & | Relationship potential |
|---|---|
| Otter | Snake will constantly be jealous of Otter's popularity and will soon seek the limelight with other, less attractive companions. |
| Hawk | Snake is patient, while Hawk is rash. Neither will be able to understand the other's behavior. They will soon depart to find more compatible companions. |
| Deer | Snake can take the hard knocks in life, while Deer has a tendency to falter. Snake will think Deer weak, and Deer will think Snake too rigid and critical. |
| Salmon | Both are quite sensual, but Salmon is openly affectionate, while Snake will only demonstrate feelings in private. Over time, they will feel uncomfortable with each other. |
| Raven | Raven will be open to manipulation and deception when Snake turns on the charisma. Snake will soon tire of the game, and Raven will feel lucky to be out of the union. |
| Owl | Owl and Snake are rivals in any context, and a relationship will bring out the worst in both of them — jealousy and deceitfulness in Snake, pride and intolerance in Owl. |
| Snake | Snake pairing with another will bring about a mirroring effect, whereby the best and the worst in each other will be magnified. |

# THE OWL

## Ideal pairings

| Owl & | Relationship potential |
|---|---|
| Hawk | Both have a strong sense of right and wrong. They will find their values match, and will be happy to live according to their principles and ethics. |
| Salmon | Both have energy to burn, and will find the other stimulating company. Salmon can gain wise counsel from Owl, while Owl will find Salmon has an exciting charm. |
| Otter | This pair will make a good match. Owl will provide wisdom and the sensible touch, while Otter will provide Owl with youthful enthusiasm. |
| Raven | Sensible Owl will encourage Raven's strong social conscience. Raven will reward Owl with influential networks and contacts. |
| Deer | **Complement.** A natural attraction and kinship exists between these two animal totems. Each will make the other a loyal and supportive companion. |

## Challenging pairings

| Owl & | Relationship potential |
|---|---|
| Snow Goose | Both will want to dominate the relationship, and antagonism will build over time. |
| Wolf | Owl will be frustrated, and intolerant of Wolf's indecisiveness and sensitivity. Wolf will soon feel it better to go it alone. |
| Beaver | Each will want to dominate the other in this relationship. Beaver will remain inflexible despite Owl's attempts to exert influence, and Owl will be too proud to give Beaver any ground. |
| Woodpecker | Owl is too self-reliant for Woodpecker, who will not feel any true union between them. Owl will not find Woodpecker stimulating company. |
| Brown Bear | These two opinionated and strong-willed individuals will clash on meeting. They will end up as adversaries in most situations. |
| Snake | Owl and Snake are rivals in any context, and a relationship will bring out the worst in both of them — jealousy and deceitfulness in Snake, and pride and intolerance in Owl. |
| Owl | Owl pairing with another will bring about a mirroring effect, whereby the best and the worst in each other will be magnified. |

# WORKING THE MEDICINE WHEEL

Animal totem astrology is an active system, one that encourages zealous exploration of the world of humans and the world of nature. American Indians have always been encouraged to experience life from all perspectives — to embrace all of the other animal totems at some point in their lives. This means consciously taking on another animal totem's perspective of life, in order to learn to appreciate its unique gifts and powers. You can use the system yourself for self-development.

Specific animal totems can be selected if you require specific powers or healing medicine. A person who has experienced and embraced the unique powers of all twelve birth totems will have learned all that is required on the conscious plane, and will be ready to be transported to a higher spiritual plane in their next life.

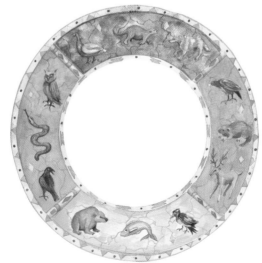

Here are the elements of the Medicine Wheel. See page 11 for a full illustration of the Wheel.

| Direction, season totem and principal element | Season | Time | Birth totem | Birth time element |
|---|---|---|---|---|
| North/White Buffalo<br>AIR | Winter | Renewal<br>Cleansing<br>Strong winds | Snow Goose<br>Otter<br>Wolf | Earth<br>Air<br>Water |
| East/Eagle<br>FIRE | Spring | Budding<br>Growing<br>Flowering | Hawk<br>Beaver<br>Deer | Fire<br>Earth<br>Air |
| South/Coyote<br>WATER | Summer | Long days<br>Ripening<br>Harvesting | Woodpecker<br>Salmon<br>Brown Bear | Water<br>Fire<br>Earth |
| West/Grizzly Bear<br>EARTH | Autumn | Falling leaves<br>Frosting<br>Long nights | Raven<br>Snake<br>Owl | Air<br>Water<br>Fire |

## The Power and Medicine of the Animal Totems

This section details for you the unique powers and medicine of each of the twelve animal totems. The power of an animal totem is what you would gain if you chose to experience life from that totem's perspective for a while. If, for example, you are enduring difficult times — ill health, stress or a negative emotional state — you can focus on a person with an animal totem different from your own. As you focus, and try to adopt the other person's life perspective, you will start to gain some of the other totem's power.

Once you have acquired an animal totem's power, you will have access to that totem's medicine. The text below tells you which animal totem to choose when you are in need of healing medicine.

For example, if you feel that you are too passive and need to take some action in your life, try to see from the perspective of a Beaver. Gather about you symbols of the Beaver, spend time with someone who has this animal totem, and get to know what the affinities in the plant and animal kingdoms are and keep them nearby.

### Hawk for LOGICAL PERSPECTIVE

*Power:* The ability to heighten your awareness, your vision, and your perception of your environment.

*Medicine:* Use when a logical or objective perspective is required rather than an emotional response.

### Beaver for HARD WORK

*Power:* The ability to appreciate material achievement through planned and methodical work.

*Medicine:* Use when action or hard work is called for.

### Deer for UNCONDITIONAL LOVE

*Power:* The ability to be gentle and gracious toward yourself, and to influence others and endear yourself to them.

*Medicine:* Use when unconditional love and acceptance are required.

### Woodpecker for INTUITION

*Power:* The ability to stay in balance and true to yourself regardless of the situation.

*Medicine:* Use when intuition is required and/or when a strong inner voice is required.

### Salmon for COURAGE

*Power:* The ability to experience fully your primal and vital energies.

*Medicine:* Use when courage, strength, leadership are called for, and/or to balance sexual urges.

### Brown Bear for TENACITY

*Power:* The ability to draw on your physical and emotional strength when required.

*Medicine:* Use when hard work, tenacity and trustworthiness are required. Use in times of adversity.

### Raven for TRANSFORMING LIFE
*Power:* The ability to inject magic and renewed faith into your life.
*Medicine:* Use when stuck in non-productive situations and/or if you want to transform a mundane life.

### Snake for EMBRACING CHANGE
*Power:* The ability to adapt easily, transform, and experience change in your life.
*Medicine:* Use when experiencing change, to enable you to stop resisting and willingly embrace the 'new.'

### Owl for SEEING CLEARLY
*Power:* The ability to see clearly in times of uncertainty, deception or political unrest.
*Medicine:* Use when facing your darkest fears or to see and understand the whole truth of a matter.

### Snow Goose for PATIENCE
*Power:* The ability to act only when the time is right.
*Medicine:* Use when patience is called for, or when you need to adhere to a set of principles while making a decision.

### Otter for FUN AND FREEDOM

*Power:* The ability to connect with your inner child, and to find joy,
passion and a sense of freedom.
*Medicine:* Use when imagination or innovation is required,
and to put fun back into your everyday life.

### Wolf for PROTECTION

*Power:* The ability to follow your instincts and intuition rather
than your intellect.
*Medicine:* Use when experiencing physical danger, or to protect others
from immediate threat.

# GLOSSARY

**active energy**  energy associated with the sun and conscious activity, linked to the elements of fire and air; the animal totems with either fire or air as their birth time element demonstrate active energy in their general behavior

**affinities**  specific minerals and plants associated with each birth time; acquiring and using them can add further strength to an animal totem's specific power and medicine

**American Indians**  earliest human inhabitants of North America

**animal totem**  animal symbol representing a birth time, season or element of nature

**birth time element**  the element of nature ruling your birth time

**birth totem**  the animal representing your birth time

**elemental clan**  the animal group you belong to, given your birth time element

**elements**  nature's forces — earth, air, fire and water

**energy flow**  energy flows through life in two complementary ways: actively and receptively. It is the flow of energy that gives force to the elements of earth, fire, air, and water. Each of the birth totems has either an active or a receptive energy flow; knowing the type will help you to understand how each totem behaves

**Medicine Wheel**  A diagram illustrating the circular motion of life — the seasons, the forces of nature, and the powerful totems and affinities associated with each season

**Native Americans**  see American Indians

**pure signs**  animal totems for which the same element — air, earth, fire or water — governs both the season and birth time: Otter is pure air, Hawk is pure fire, and Woodpecker is pure water; no animal totem is pure earth

**receptive energy**  energy associated with the moon and unconscious activity; linked to the elements of earth and water. The animal totems with either earth or water as their birth time element demonstrate receptive energy in their general behavior

**season element**  the element ruling the season in which a person is born; sometimes referred to as the 'principal element'

**season totem**  the animal totem representing the season in which a person is born; sometimes referred to as the 'directional totem'

**shaman**  tribal wise man or holy man with the power and skills to interpret the messages between the spirit and natural worlds and among the animal, mineral and plant kingdoms

# Reading More about American Indian Culture & Astrology

Bryant, Page, *The Aquarian Guide To Native American Mythology*, The Aquarian Press/HarperCollins, London, 1991.

Kennedy, Mike Dixon, *Native American Myth & Legend*, Blandford/Cassell, London, 1996.

Lawson, David, *So You want to be a Shaman*, Conari Press & Publishers Group West, California, 1996.

McNeese, Tim, *Illustrated Myths of Native America*, Blandford/Cassell, London, 1998.

Meadows, Kenneth, *The Little Library of Earth Medicine*, Dorling Kindersley Limited, London, 1998.

Mengelkoch, L. & Nerburn, K., *Native American Wisdom*, New World Library, San Rafael, California, 1991.

Moondance, Wolf, *Spirit Medicine*, Sterling Publishing Company, New York, 1995.

Rain, Mary Summer, *Earthway*, Pocket Books, New York, 1990.

Sams, Jamie & Carson, David, *Medicine Cards*, Bear & Company, Santa Fe, New Mexico, 1988.

Sun Bear & Wabun, *The Medicine Wheel: Earth Astrology*, Fireside/Simon & Schuster, New York, 1982.

Sun Bear, Wabun, Wind & Mulligan, Crysalis, *Dancing with the Wheel*, *The Medicine Wheel Workbook*, Fireside/Simon & Schuster, New York, 1992.

Wherry, Joseph H., *The Totem Pole Indians*, Wilfred Funk, Inc., New York, 1964.

# INDEX OF ANIMAL NAMES

Note: **bold type** denotes a section devoted to that animal.

Published by Lansdowne Publishing Pty Ltd
Sydney NSW 2001, Australia

Commissioned by Deborah Nixon
Production Manager: Sally Stokes
Text: Debbie Burns
Illustration: Penny Lovelock
Design: Sue Rawkins
Editor: Avril Janks
Graphic illustrations: Sue Rawkins
Project Co-ordinator: Kate Merrifield

National Library of Australia Cataloguing-in-Publication-Data

Burns, Debbie, 1962-.

Animal totem astrology.

ISBN 1 86302 762 2.

1. Indian astrology. 2. Totems.
3. Animals. I. Title.

133.59397

This book is intended to give general information only. The publishers
expressly disclaim all liability to any person arising directly or indirectly from
the use of, or for any errors or omissions in, the information in this book. The
adoption and application of the information in this book is at the reader's
discretion and is his or her sole responsibility.

Set in Stempel Schneidler, GoudySans Book and Fajita on QuarkXPress
Printed in Singapore by Tien Wah Press (Pte) Ltd